Br

**Cards**

**Annelies Karduks**

FORTE PUBLISHERS

# Contents

ISBN 90 5877 511 9

This is a publication from
Forte Publishers BV
P.O. Box 1394
3500 BJ Utrecht
The Netherlands

For more information about the creative books available from Forte Uitgevers:
www.forteuitgevers.nl

Final editing: Gina Kors-Lambers, Steenwijk, the Netherlands
Photography and digital image editing:
Fotografie Gerhard Witteveen, Apeldoorn, the Netherlands
Cover and inner design:
BADE creatieve communicatie, Baarn, the Netherlands
Translation: Michael Ford, TextCase, Hilversum, the Netherlands

# Preface

The brodery templates combine two popular techniques, namely embossing and embroidery. The series of materials consists of two rulers, two semicircles and two triangles. The templates contain several embroidery patterns and each template also has a special cutting edge. In order to make this concept complete, special brodery patterned sheets have been designed which match the embossing patterns on the templates. In this book, I will explain in detail the many possibilities offered by these templates and patterned sheets. I wish you many hours of fun.

See page 32 if you wish to remain informed of what I have in store for you in the future.

Have fun.

Annelies Karduks

I wish to thank Cynthia Kamphorst for helping me to embroider the cards.

# Techniques

Read these instructions carefully and look at the Step-by-step photographs before you start. Always work carefully when making these cards.

## Cutting

Use non-permanent adhesive tape to stick the template on the embossing card. Cut the border or the shape and move the template where necessary.

## Embossing

Stick the brodery template, together with the embossing card, onto a light box. Emboss (part of) the pattern by copying the shapes which are lit using an embossing stylus. Where necessary, move the card to emboss the rest of the pattern. If you wish, you can use Pergasoft to make the embossing easier.

## Pricking

Turn the embossed card and the template over and place them on a pricking mat. Choose a pattern and prick the holes using the extra fine perforating tool. Repeat this pattern as often as necessary. Use the fine perforating tool to prick holes where more than one thread is thread through. Look at the back to see whether all the necessary holes have been pricked. If necessary, place a tool grip around the perforating tool.

## Embroidery

Thread the thread through the card from the back to the front and use adhesive tape to stick it to the back of the card, but not on the pattern. Embroider the pattern. Make sure the threads run tightly over the card and, when finished, attach the thread to the back of the card again using adhesive tape. If necessary, close the holes at the back of the card.

*Tip: Where necessary, draw pencil lines and use these, together with the guide lines, the guide cross and the guide dot in the templates, to mirror the shape or pattern, to cut the shape into a number of pieces, to find the middle of the card, etc.*

## Star pattern

Copy the pattern twice and cut them out leaving a border. Use Pritt On & Off to stick the pattern on a piece of card and cut out the desired star size.

# Materials

- Card and paper: cArt-us (CA), Mi-Teintes Canson (C) and Papicolor (P) (the colour number is stated for every type of card)
- Brodery templates 1 to 6
- Brodery sheets 1 to 8
- Template tape
- 3M Scotch Removable Magic Tape
- Adhesive tape
- Light box
- Fiskars embossing tool (small tip)
- Perforating tool (extra fine)
- Perforating tool (fine)
- Tool grip
- Pricking mat
- Pearl needles
- Propelling pencil
- Rubber
- Pritt On & Off
- Scoring pen
- Cutting ruler with a metal edge
- Cutting mat
- Hobby knife
- Tweezer scissors
- 3D cutting sheets
- Photo glue
- 3D foam tape/blocks of foam tape and/or 3D glue
- Eyelet tool
- Eyelet hammer
- Circle cutter

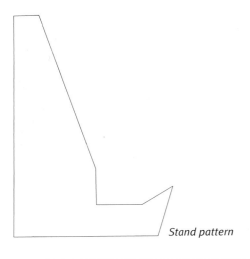

Stand pattern

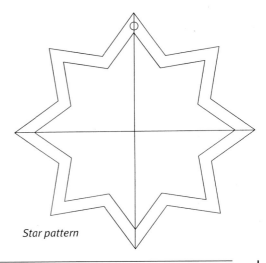

Star pattern

# Step-by-step

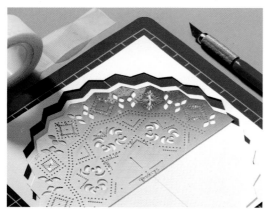

Cutting

Embossing

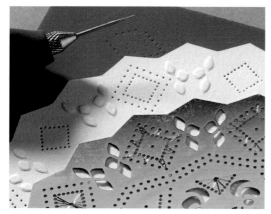

Pricking

Embroidering

# Round card (card on the cover)

## What you need

- cArt-us card: green 367 (P 16)
- Mi-Teintes card: white 335
- Brodery template 4
- Stand pattern
- Picturel step-by-step cutting sheet: dahlias
- Sulky thread: dark pink 7013 and Christmas green 7018
- Adhesive stones: fuchsia
- Decoration chalks
- Pritt On & Off

## Method

1. Cut a white card (14 x 14 cm) and draw a cross on the back in the middle of the card.

2. Stick the brodery template on the square so that the guide dot is exactly in the middle of the cross you have drawn.

3. Follow the general instructions for the cutting, embossing, pricking and embroidery. Combine the first and second pattern from the right.

4. Cut two green circles (Ø 13.5 cm and Ø 8 cm) and a white circle (Ø 7 cm).

5. Apply decoration chalk to the edge of the white circle.

6. Copy the pattern of the stand and cut it out leaving a border.

7. Use Pritt On & Off to stick the pattern on green card and cut out the stand.

8. Stick the decorated white circle on the green circle.

9. Stick fuchsia adhesive stones and 3D dahlias on the front of the card.

# Sea world

## Orange fish

**What you need**

- *cArt-us card: dark blue 417 (P 41) and cornflower blue 393 (P 05)*
- *Brodery template 1*
- *Brodery sheet 4 (blue/light blue)*
- *Picturel cutting sheet: coral fish/shells*
- *Sulky thread: blue 7016*
- *Adhesive stones: orange*
- *Funny ribbons: assorted yellow/salmon/brown*

**Method**

1. Cut, score and fold a dark blue double card (10.5 x 14.8 cm).

2. Cut a cornflower blue rectangle (10.5 x 14.8 cm) and mark the middle of the long side.

3. Place the brodery template 2 mm inside the edge of the card so that the middle of the template is level with the middle of the long side of the cornflower blue rectangle.

4. Follow the general instructions for the cutting, embossing, pricking and embroidering using the first pattern from the right.

5. Cut a rectangle (8 x 15 cm) out of the brodery sheet and a cut a dark blue rectangle (7 x 15 cm).

6. Stick everything on the card and carefully cut the edges of the rectangles to the size of the card. Stick a self-adhesive ribbon and 3D fish on the front of the card.

7. Decorate the card with orange adhesive stones.

# Two fish

## What you need

- cArt-us card: dark blue 417 (P 41) and cornflower blue 393 (P 05)
- Mi-Teintes card: azure 102
- Brodery template 2
- Brodery sheet 5 (blue/yellow)
- Picturel cutting sheet: coral fish/shells
- Sulky thread: blue 7016 and peacock blue 7052
- Funny ribbons: assorted yellow/salmon/brown

## Method

1. Cut, score and fold a dark blue double card (10.5 x 14.8 cm).

2. Cut an azure rectangle (10.5 x 14.8 cm) and mark the middle of the two short sides.

3. Place the brodery template 2 mm inside the edge of the card so that the middle of the template is level with the middle of the short side of the azure rectangle.

4. Follow the general instructions for the cutting, embossing, pricking and embroidering of both sides. Make sure two embroidery patterns and two different colours of thread are used.

5. Cut a cornflower blue rectangle (9 x 11 cm), a rectangle (8 x 11 cm) out of the brodery sheet and a dark blue rectangle (6 x 11 cm). Stick the rectangles on top of each other.

6. Stick everything on the card and carefully cut the edges of the rectangles to the size of the card.

7. Stick self-adhesive ribbon and 3D fish on the front of the card.

# Fish with a shell

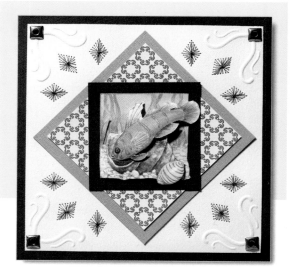

## What you need

- cArt-us card: dark blue 417 (P 41) and cornflower blue 393 (P 05)
- Mi-Teintes card: azure 102
- Brodery template 5
- Brodery sheet 4 (blue/light blue)
- Picturel cutting sheet: coral fish/shells
- Sulky thread: peacock blue 7052
- Metallic fun eyelet shapes: light blue

## Method

1. Cut, score and fold a dark blue double card (13.5 x 13.5 cm).

2. Cut an azure square (12 x 12 cm).

3. Stick the brodery template on a light box. Place the azure square on top so that the corner of the azure square is level with the inner corner of holes.

4. Follow the general instructions for the embossing, pricking and embroidering.

5. Use the small diamond of the first pattern from the right. Do the same for all four corners.

6. Cut a cornflower blue square (8 x 8 cm), a square (7 x 7 cm) from the brodery sheet and a dark blue rectangle (5.7 x 5.7 cm).

7. Stick everything on the card.

8. Stick a 3D fish on the front of the card.

9. Decorate the card with eyelets.

# Thank you

**What you need**

- cArt-us card: dark blue 417 (P 41) and cornflower blue 393 (P 05)
- Mi-Teintes card: azure 102
- Brodery template 3
- Picturel cutting sheet: coral fish/shells
- Sulky thread: blue 7016
- Eyelets: clear aquarelle
- Eyelet handwriting letters
- Alphabet punch
- Adhesive stones: dark blue
- Sticker sheet: silver 1033

## Method

1. Cut, score and fold a dark blue double card (13.5 x 13.5 cm).

2. Cut an azure square (14 x 14 cm) and draw a cross on the back in the middle of the square.

3. Stick the brodery template on the square so that the guide dot is exactly in the middle of the cross that you have just drawn.

4. Follow the general instructions for the cutting, embossing, pricking and embroidering. Make sure two different embroidery patterns are used.

5. Cut a dark blue circle (Ø 9 cm).

6. Use eyelets to attach the letters to the circle.

7. Stick the circles on the card.

8. Stick punched letters and corner stickers on the front of the card.

9. Add some 3D shells and decorate the card with dark blue adhesive stones.

# Roses

## Rose

### What you need

- cArt-us card: old red 517 (P 12) and salmon 482 (P 05)
- Brodery template 6
- Brodery sheet 8 (red/pink)
- Picturel cutting sheet: roses/hearts
- Sulky thread: Christmas red 7014

### Method

1. Cut, score and fold an old red double card (13.5 x 13.5 cm).

2. Cut a salmon square (14 x 14 cm) and draw a diagonal cross on the back.

3. Place the guide dot of the brodery template in the middle of the cross.

4. Follow the general instructions for the cutting, embossing, pricking and embroidering using the first pattern from the left.

5. Cut two old red squares (8.5 x 8.5 cm and 6 x 6 cm) and a square (8 x 8 cm) out of the brodery sheet.

6. Stick the squares on top of each other.

7. Stick everything on the card.

8. Stick a 3D rose on the front of the card.

# W&A

## What you need

- cArt-us card: old red 517 (P 12) and salmon 482 (P 05)
- Brodery template 1
- Brodery sheet 8 (red/pink)
- Picturel cutting sheet: roses/hearts
- Sulky thread: Christmas red 7014
- Eyelet handwriting letters
- Sizzix die cutter
- Sizzix die: double heart
- Bradletz: salmon

## Method

1. Cut, score and fold an old red double card (10.5 x 14.8 cm).

2. Cut a salmon rectangle (10.5 x 14.8 cm) and mark the middle of the two long sides.

3. Place the brodery template 2 mm inside the edge of the card so that the middle of the template is level with the middle of the long side of the salmon rectangle.

4. Follow the general instructions for the cutting, embossing, pricking and embroidering of both sides using the third pattern from the right.

5. Cut a rectangle (5 x 15 cm) out of the brodery sheet and an old red rectangle (4 x 15 cm).

6. Stick the rectangles on top of each other.

7. Stick everything on the card and carefully cut the edges of the rectangles to the size of the card.

8. Use Bradletz to attach the punched shape and the letters to the card.

9. Stick 3D hearts on the front of the card.

# With love

## What you need

- cArt-us card: old red 517 (P 12) and salmon 482 (P 05)
- Brodery template 5
- Brodery sheet 8 (red/pink)
- Picturel cutting sheet: roses/hearts
- Sulky thread: Christmas red 7014
- Coluzzle template, knife and cutting mat
- Tagged vellum flower
- Bradletz: salmon
- Letter beads
- Funny Fibres: assorted red/orange/pink

## Method

1. Cut, score and fold an old red double card (10.5 x 14.8 cm).

2. Cut a salmon rectangle (10.5 x 14.8 cm) and draw the long middle line on the back.

3. Place the brodery template against the edge of the salmon rectangle with the point and the guide dot on the middle line that you have just drawn.

4. Follow the general instructions for the cutting, embossing, pricking and embroidering using the small diamond of the first pattern from the right. Prick the large diamond for decoration.

5. Cut out the label and place the brodery template with a diamond in the middle 1 cm from the bottom of the label. Repeat step 4.

6. Cut two 1 cm wide strips from the brodery sheet and stick them on the card.

7. Use Bradletz to stick the label and the tagged flower on the card.

8. Use foam tape or 3D glue to stick the picture on the card.

9. Stick the letters on the card with Funny Fibres.

# Rose bouquet

## What you need

- cArt-us card: old red 517 (P 12) and salmon 482 (P 05)
- Brodery template 4
- Brodery sheet 8 (red/pink)
- Picturel cutting sheet: roses/hearts
- Sulky thread: Christmas red 7014
- Tagged vellum circle
- Funny Fibres: assorted red/orange/pink
- Adhesive stones: red
- Mini eyelet rings (silver)

## Method

1. Cut, score and fold a salmon double card (13.5 x 13.5 cm) and draw a diagonal cross inside the card.

2. Place the guide dot of the brodery template in the middle of the cross.

3. Follow the general instructions for the cutting, embossing, pricking and embroidering using the second pattern from the right.

4. Cut an old red square (13.5 x 13.5 cm) and stick it behind the salmon card.

5. Cut a square (13 x 13 cm) out of the brodery sheet and cut it diagonally in two. Stick this on the front of the card.

6. Cut two old red circles (Ø 8.5 cm and Ø 4.3 cm).

7. Use an eyelet to attach the tagged circle to the smallest circle. Use foam tape or 3D glue to stick the picture on the card.

8. Stick the other parts on the card.

9. Use Funny Fibres to hang the tag on the card.

10. Decorate the card with 3D roses and red heart adhesive stones.

# Anemones and gerberas

## Pink anemones

### What you need

- cArt-us card: lilac 453 (P 14)
- Mi-Teintes card: white 335
- Brodery template 3
- Brodery sheet 3 (lilac/green)
- Scrapbook stitches: watercolor brite
- Shake It step-by-step cutting sheet: anemones

### Method

1. Cut, score and fold a lilac double card (13.5 x 13.5 cm).

2. Cut a white square (12 x 12 cm) and draw a cross on the back in the middle of the card.

3. Place the brodery template on the card with the smooth side against the side of the square and with the guide dot on the middle line.

4. Follow the general instructions for the embossing, pricking and embroidering using half of the second pattern from the right. Move the brodery template four times.

5. Cut a square (13 x 13 cm) out of the brodery sheet and cut a lilac rectangle (12 x 12 cm).

6. Cut 2 mm off of each side of the embroidered square.

7. Stick everything on the card.

8. Stick 3D anemones on the front of the card.

# Purple anemone

**Method**

1. Cut, score and fold a lilac double card (10.5 x 14.8 cm).

2. Cut a white rectangle (10.5 x 14.8 cm) and place the brodery template in the corner.

3. Follow the general instructions for the cutting, embossing, pricking and embroidering using the second and third patterns from the left. Move the template where necessary.

4. Cut a rectangle (8 x 13 cm) out of the brodery sheet and cut a lilac rectangle (7 x 12 cm).

5. Stick the lilac rectangle on the rectangle cut out of the brodery sheet and stick this on the card.

6. Carefully cut the edges of the rectangles to the size of the card.

7. Stick 3D anemones on the front of the card.

**What you need**

- cArt-us card: lilac 453 (P 14)
- Mi-Teintes card: white 335
- Brodery template 5
- Brodery sheet 3 (lilac/green)
- Scrapbook stitches: watercolor brite
- Shake It step-by-step cutting sheet: anemones

# Gerbera

## What you need

- *cArt-us card: spring green 305 (P 08)*
- *Mi-Teintes card: white 335*
- *Brodery template 4*
- *Scrapbook stitches: watercolor brite*
- *Eyelets: clear aquarelle*
- *Shake It step-by-step cutting sheet: gerberas*

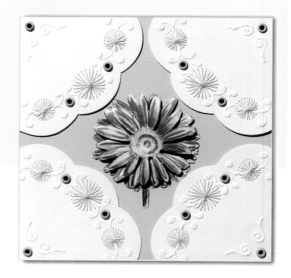

## Method

1. Cut, score and fold a spring green double card (13.5 x 13.5 cm).

2. Cut a white square (14 x 14 cm) and draw a cross on the back in the middle of the card.

3. Place the brodery template on the card with the guide lines and guide dot on the cross.

4. Follow the general instructions for the cutting, embossing and pricking.

5. Cut the shape in four along the lines of the cross.

6. Use the first pattern from the right for both the large and the medium-sized circles. Use thread of two different colours.

7. Use the same template to emboss the corners.

8. Stick everything on the card.

9. Decorate the card with eyelets.

10. Stick a 3D gerbera on the front of the card.

# Larissa

## What you need

- cArt-us card: spring green 305 (P 08)
- Mi-Teintes card: white 335
- Brodery template 2
- Scrapbook stitches: watercolor brite
- Eyelets: clear aquarelle
- Eyelet handwriting letters
- Shake It step-by-step cutting sheet: Little flowers (anemones/gerberas)

## Method

1. Cut, score and fold a spring green double card (10.5 x 14.8 cm).

2. Cut a white rectangle (10.5 x 14.8 cm) and mark the middle of the two long sides.

3. Place the brodery template 2 mm inside the edge of the card so that the middle of the template is level with the middle of the long side of the white rectangle.

4. Follow the general instructions for the cutting, embossing, pricking and embroidering of both sides. Note: use the second pattern from the right for both the small and the large square and use two different colours of thread.

5. Cut a spring green rectangle (4.5 x 14.8 cm) and stick it on the card.

6. Place the letters on the card and mark where the eyelets must go. Use eyelets to attach the letters.

7. Stick 3D gerberas on the front of the card.

# Fruit

## Blossom

### What you need

- cArt-us card: old red 517 (P 12)
- Mi-Teintes card: lime 100
- Brodery template 2
- Brodery sheet 7 (red/apple green)
- Picturel cutting sheet: forest fruit/border
- Sulky thread: Christmas red 7014
- Bradletz: dark green squares

### Method

1. Cut, score and fold an old red double card (10.5 x 14.8 cm).

2. Cut a lime rectangle (9.5 x 14.8 cm) and mark the middle of the long side.

3. Place the middle of the brodery template level with the middle of the lime rectangle.

4. Follow the general instructions for the pricking and embroidering using the second pattern from the left. Also prick the middle dot of the pattern.

5. Cut a rectangle (7 x 15 cm) out of the brodery sheet and cut an old red rectangle (6 x 9 cm).

6. Stick everything on the card and carefully cut the edges of the rectangle to the size of the card.

7. Stick 3D fruit on the front of the card.

8. Attach the Bradletz to the pricked middle dots.

# Berries

## What you need
- cArt-us card: old red 517 (P 12)
- Mi-Teintes card: lime 100
- Brodery template 3
- Brodery sheet 7 (red/apple green)
- Picturel cutting sheet: forest fruit/border
- Sulky thread: Christmas red 7014
- Adhesive stones: light green

## Method

1. Cut, score and fold an old red double card (13.5 x 13.5 cm).

2. Cut a lime square (13.5 x 13.5 cm) and draw a cross on the back in the middle of the card.

3. Place the guide dot of the brodery template in the middle of the cross.

4. Follow the general instructions for the cutting, embossing, pricking and embroidering. Make sure two different embroidery patterns are used.

5. Cut three strips (1 x 14 cm) from the brodery sheet.

6. Cut an old red circle (Ø 9 cm).

7. Stick everything on the card and carefully cut the edges of the strips to the size of the card.

8. Stick 3D fruit on the front of the card.

9. Decorate the card with light green adhesive stones.

# Strawberries

## What you need

- cArt-us card: old red 517 (P 12)
- Mi-Teintes card: lime 100 and apple green 475
- Brodery template 5
- Brodery sheet 7 (red/apple green)
- Picturel cutting sheet: forest fruit/border
- Sulky thread: Christmas red 7014
- Safety pins
- Metal embroidery label: square

## Method

1. Cut, score and fold an old red double card (13.5 x 13.5 cm).

2. Cut a salmon square (14 x 14 cm) and draw a diagonal cross on the back.

3. Place the guide dot of the brodery template in the middle of the cross.

4. Follow the general instructions for the cutting, embossing, pricking and embroidering using the first pattern from the left.

5. Cut an apple green square (8.5 x 8.5 cm), a square (8 x 8 cm) out of the brodery sheet and an old red square (7 x 7 cm).

6. Stick the squares on top of each other.

7. Stick everything on the card and stick 3D fruit on the front of the card.

8. Cut two old red squares (3 x 3 cm) and two squares (2 x 2 cm) out of the brodery sheet.

9. Stick the squares together with the embroidery labels between the squares.

10. Thread three threads through the top hole.

11. Tie the threads together and use a safety pin to attach them to the card.

# Forest fruit

## What you need

- cArt-us card: old red 517 (P 12)
- Mi-Teintes card: lime 100 and apple green 475
- Brodery template 6
- Brodery sheet 7 (red/apple green)
- Picturel cutting sheet: forest fruit/border
- Sulky thread: Christmas red 7014
- Bradletz: dark green squares
- Coluzzle template tiny tags, knife and cutting mat.
- Glass sticker: medium oval
- Eyelets: soft aquarelle
- Satin ribbon: olive green

## Method

1. Cut, score and fold an old red double card (13.5 x 13.5 cm).

2. Cut a lime square (12 x 12 cm).

3. Stick the brodery template on a light box. Place the lime square on top so that the corner of the lime square is level with the inner corner of holes.

4. Follow the general instructions for the embossing, pricking and embroidering of the four corners using the middle of the top pattern.

5. Cut two squares (13 x 13 cm and 6 x 6 cm) out of the brodery sheet, cut an apple green square (7 x 7 cm) and an old red square (4 x 4 cm).

6. Stick everything on the card and stick 3D fruit on the front of the card.

7. Cut the labels. Place the template with an oval in the middle on the labels and repeat step 4.

8. Use an eyelet to attach the labels together and stick a glass sticker on the top label.

9. Use a satin ribbon and a Bradletz to attach the labels to the card. Add the other Bradletz to the card.

# Flowers and butterflies

## Bunch of roses

### What you need

- cArt-us card: aqua blue 427 (P 06)
- Mi-Teintes card: bright yellow 400
- Brodery template 5
- Scrapbook stitches: watercolor brite
- Picturel cutting sheet: flowers/butterflies

### Method

1. Cut, score and fold an aqua blue double card (10.5 x 14.8 cm).

2. Cut a yellow rectangle (10.5 x 14.8 cm) and draw the long middle line on the back.

3. Place the brodery template against the edge of the yellow rectangle with the point and the guide dot on the middle line.

4. Follow the general instructions for the cutting, embossing, pricking and embroidering of both sides using the second pattern from the right.

5. Cut an aqua blue square (5.8 x 5.8 cm).

6. Stick everything on the card.

7. Stick 3D flowers and a 3D butterfly on the front of the card.

# Robine

## What you need

- cArt-us card: aqua blue 427 (P 06)
- Mi-Teintes card: bright yellow 400
- Brodery template 6
- Scrapbook stitches: watercolor brite
- Picturel cutting sheet: flowers/butterflies
- Marjoleine scrapbook sheet: blue alphabet
- Bradletz: dark blue

## Method

1. Cut, score and fold an aqua blue double card (10.5 x 14.8 cm).

2. Cut a yellow rectangle (10.5 x 14.8 cm) and mark the middle of the two long sides.

3. Place the brodery template 2 mm inside the edge of the card so that the middle of the embossing template is level with the middle of the long side of the yellow rectangle.

4. Follow the general instructions for the cutting, embossing, pricking and embroidering of both sides using the top pattern in the middle. Move the template where necessary and also prick the middle dot in the patterns.

5. Cut an aqua blue rectangle (6 x 15 cm) and a yellow rectangle (1.5 cm x 1.5 cm) and stick them on the card.

6. Carefully cut the edges of the rectangles to the size of the card.

7. Attach the Bradletz in the pricked holes.

8. Decorate the card with the letters.

9. Use 3D glue or foam tape to stick the flowers and the butterflies on the card.

# Aster

## What you need

- cArt-us card: aqua blue 427 (P 06)
- Mi-Teintes card: bright yellow 400
- Brodery template 4
- Brodery sheet 6 (dark blue/yellow)
- Scrapbook stitches: watercolor brite
- Picturel cutting sheet: flowers/butterflies

## Method

1. Cut, score and fold an aqua blue double card (13.5 x 13.5 cm).

2. Cut a yellow square (12 x 12 cm) and draw a cross on the back in the middle of the card.

3. Place the smooth side of the brodery template against the side of the square with the guide dot on the middle line.

4. Follow the general instructions for the embossing, pricking and embroidering using the top pattern in the middle. Move the brodery template four times.

5. Cut a square (13 x 13 cm) out of the brodery sheet and two aqua blue squares (12 x 12 cm and 5 x 5 cm).

6. Cut 2 mm off of each side of the embroidered square.

7. Stick everything on the card.

8. Stick a 3D picture of a flower and a butterfly on the front of the card.

# Rose

## What you need

- cArt-us card: aqua blue 427 (P 06)
- Mi-Teintes card: bright yellow 400
- Brodery template 2
- Brodery sheet 6 (dark blue/yellow)
- Scrapbook stitches: watercolor brite
- Picturel cutting sheet: flowers/butterflies

## Method

1. Cut, score and fold an aqua blue double card (13.5 x 13.5 cm).

2. Cut a yellow square (12 x 12 cm) and draw a diagonal cross on the back. Draw a line 3.2 cm from each corner.

3. Place the brodery template on the card with the top edge on the line and the guide cross on the line of the cross.

4. Follow the general instructions for the cutting, embossing, pricking and embroidering using the first pattern from the right. Move the brodery template four times.

5. Cut a square (13 x 13 cm) out of the brodery sheet and cut two aqua blue squares (12 x 12 cm and 5.5 x 5.5 cm).

6. Stick everything on the card.

7. Stick a 3D picture of a flower and a butterfly on the front of the card.

# Christmas

## Candles

### What you need

- cArt-us card: dark red 519 (P 43)
- Mi-Teintes card: ivory 111
- Brodery template 3
- Brodery sheet 1 (green/red)
- Sulky thread: red/gold/green 7027
- Nel van Veen step-by-step cutting sheet: Christmas lantern
- Mine eyelet rings (gold)

### Method

1. Cut, score and fold a dark red double card (13.5 x 13.5 cm).

2. Cut an ivory square (14 x 14 cm) and draw a cross on the back in the middle of the card.

3. Place the brodery template on the card with the guide lines and guide dot on the cross.

4. Follow the general instructions for the cutting, embossing and pricking.

5. Cut the shape in four along the lines of the cross.

6. Embroider the pattern using the third pattern from the right.

7. Cut two squares (4 x 4 cm) out of the brodery sheet and cut them diagonally in two.

8. Stick everything on the card.

9. Decorate the card with eyelets and a 3D candle.

# Star on a circle

## Method

1. Cut, score and fold a dark red double card (10.5 x 14.8 cm).

2. Cut an ivory rectangle (10.5 x 14.8 cm) and draw the long middle line on the back.

3. Place the brodery template against the edge of the rectangle with the guide dot on the middle line.

4. Follow the general instructions for the cutting, embossing, pricking and embroidering of both sides combining the first pattern from the left with the first pattern from the right.

5. Cut an ivory square (9 x 9 cm). Draw a cross on the back in the middle of the card and use a circle cutter to cut out a circle (Ø 7.8 cm).

6. Place the brodery template on the card with the guide lines and the guide dot on the cross.

7. Follow the general instructions for the embossing, pricking and embroidering.

8. Cut a dark red circle (Ø 8.8 cm).

9. Stick everything on the card.

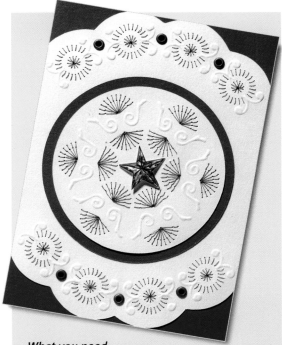

## What you need

- cArt-us card: dark red 519 (P 43)
- Mi-Teintes card: ivory 111
- Brodery template 4
- Quadrant cutting sheet: Christmas yellow/green
- Sulky thread: Christmas red 7055 and Christmas green 7018
- Metallic fun eyelet shapes (red)

10. Decorate the card with eyelets. Use 3D glue or foam tape to stick the star on the card.

# Christmas tree on a star

## What you need
- cArt-us card: dark red 519 (P 43)
- Mi-Teintes card: ivory 111
- Brodery templates 5 and 6 and brodery sheet 1 (green/red)
- Quadrant cutting sheet: Christmas yellow/green
- Sulky thread: red/gold/green 7027
- Star pattern
- Letter beads and olive green satin ribbon
- Mini eyelet rings (gold)

## Method

1. Cut, score and fold a dark red double card (10.5 x 14.8 cm).

2. Cut an ivory rectangle (10.5 x 14.8 cm) and draw the long middle line on the back.

3. Place brodery template 5 against the edge of the ivory rectangle with the guide dot on the middle line.

4. Follow the general instructions for the cutting, embossing, pricking and embroidering using the third pattern from the left.

5. Use the inner star (see page 5) to cut the ivory star. Draw a cross on the back in the middle of the card.

6. Place the brodery template on the card with the guide lines and the guide dot on the cross. Repeat step 4.

7. Use the outer star pattern to cut the red star.

8. Stick everything on the card and add some eyelets.

9. Cut two strips (1 x 11 cm) out of the brodery sheet on the card and carefully cut the edges of the strips to the size of the card.

10. Use satin ribbon to attach the letters to the card. Use 3D glue or foam tape to stick the Christmas tree on the card.

# Lantern

### What you need
- *cArt-us card: dark red 519 (P 43)*
- *Mi-Teintes card: ivory 111*
- *Brodery template* ❧
- *Brodery sheet 1 (green/red)*
- *Sulky thread: cherry red 7055*
- *Nel van Veen step-by-step cutting sheet: Christmas lantern*

### Method
1. Cut, score and fold a dark red double card (13.5 x 13.5 cm).

2. Cut an ivory square (12 x 12 cm) and draw a diagonal cross on the back. Draw a line 2.6 cm from each corner.

3. Place the brodery template on the card with the top edge against the line and the guide cross on the line of the cross.

4. Follow the general instructions for the cutting, embossing, pricking and embroidering using the third pattern from the left. Move the brodery template four times.

5. Cut a square (13 x 13 cm) out of the brodery sheet and cut two dark red squares (12 x 12 cm and 6 x 6 cm).

6. Stick everything on the card.

7. Stick a 3D lantern on the front of the card.

# Bouquet

### Method

1. Cut, score and fold an orange double card (10.5 x 14.8 cm).

2. Cut white rectangle (10.5 x 14.8 cm) and place the brodery template in the corner.

3. Follow the general instructions for the cutting, embossing, pricking and embroidering. Move the template where necessary.

4. Cut a rectangle (8 x 13 cm) out of the brodery sheet and cut an orange rectangle (7 x 12 cm).

5. Stick the orange rectangle on the rectangle cut out of the brodery sheet and stick this on the card.

6. Carefully cut the edges of the rectangles to the size of the card.

7. Decorate the card with eyelets. Add a 3D bouquet to the front of the card.

### What you need

- cArt-us card: orange 545 (P 11)
- Mi-Teintes card: white 335
- Brodery template 6
- Brodery sheet 2
- Scrapbook stitches: watercolor brite
- Eyelets: clear aquarelle
- Picturel step-by-step cutting sheet: bouquet

Many thanks to Kars & Co. B.V. in Ochten, the Netherlands, Papicolor B.V. in Utrecht, the Netherlands and Hobbyzaak Crealies in Amersfoort, the Netherlands, for providing the materials.
The materials can also be ordered from Crealies in Amersfoort, the Netherlands. (+31 (0)33 4564052 until 5.00 p.m.). The shop is open by telephone appointment. E-mail: info@crealies.nl. Also see www.crealies.nl.
Please complete the form on the website if you wish to remain informed of all the new products I have designed.